soul wide shut:

the introspective love collection

a compilation of poetic works

soul wide shut:

the introspective love collection

m. elayne bowden

soulwideshut.blogspot.com

Published by SunShyneOrygynals Press
2125 S. Andrews Circle
Columbus, Georgia 31903

FIRST EDITION

Cover Design and Book Concept by M. Elayne Bowden.

Library of Congress Cataloging-in-Publication Data

Bowden, M. Elayne
      soul wide shut : the introspective love collection/
      M. Elayne Bowden.— 1st ed.
      p. cm.
      1.   African American women—poetry. I. Title

ISBN 978-0-6151-4751-2

acknowledgements

My heartfelt gratitude and deepest appreciation go out to:

The Creator, God, my Daddy for my many blessings, lessons, and life experiences. You are so awesome. So magnificent. So loving. So faithful. Thank you for giving me the gift of creativity, and for ceaselessly granting me favor, grace and mercy. I cannot do anything without you!

My mother: Catherine Bowden for instilling in me, at a young age, a love of words, for your unconditional love, support, guidance and wisdom. You are a virtuous and phenomenal woman. I want to be just like you when I grow up!

My sister and brother by blood: Ramona Ellis and David Bowden for being my #1 fans and strongest supporters.

My other mother: Zella Cochran for loving me like I am your own and for being the first person to want (and receive) a framed copy of one of my poems.

My sisters by love: Shandra Smith, Trina Peterson, Jennifer Jones, Korie Hailstock, Darlene Williams, and Chaka Russell for your love, friendship, advice, constant prayers and encouragement.

My forever friend and self-proclaimed manager: Belinda F. McNeil for ceaselessly supporting my creative endeavors. You may have spoken this book into existence long before I knew I wanted to publish it!

My advanced readers and quasi-editors: C.L. Russell, Verronda Spivey and Xavier Pierre, Jr. for the excellent feedback and for selflessly lending your time and support to this project.

My newfound friends: Cheri Flynn and Tazwell Franklin III for being incredibly patient and extremely understanding sounding boards.

My Blogger Babies a.k.a. "The Sisterhood": **OneFromPhilly, BluJewel** (Is It Just Me?), **BZ** (Stream of Consciousness), **T.C.** (Golden Time of The Day), **Honey Libra** (Life Through My Eyes), and **ConsistentlyInconsistent** (Consistently Inconsistent) for reaching out, showing love and sharing yourselves with me. Our "kinnections" defy fiber optics and the World Wide Web!

My Blogger Peeps: **Royce's Daughter** (Proud To Be a Black Man's Daughter), **Organized Noise** (The Evolution of Organized Noise), **Rashan Jamal** (Beats, Rhymes and Life), **Shelle** (These Poets Are Crazy), **Isis** (Her

Story), **Sojourner G** (The Sojourner), **Shai** (Drawn 2 Words), and **Urban Butterfly** (Urban Butterfly) for stopping by to just read, and/or taking the time to comment favorably on my poems, not quite poems, rants and ramblings.

You, the reader: for taking the time to share this journey and for opening yourselves up to experience love from my poetic perspective.

All the Internet poetry sites I've ever called home: for making it possible to share my work and for allowing me to cultivate positive and lasting friendships with other poets and lovers of poetry.

All the men I've loved before: past, present, and future for inspiring me to think and feel in poetics.

soul wide shut is dedicated to:

The loving memory of
William Bowden,
my father and my sunshine.
Your love continues to
flow through our lives.

The beautiful memory of
Benita Norine Miles,
my sister/friend/confidante, guardian angel,
and the first person to read my poetry.

I miss you both. Every day.

contents

introduction

Dear Reader,

I appreciate you so much for taking a moment out of your life to embrace a part of mine. This project is truly an offering from my heart to every person who has ever said to me, "*you should write a book!*" or asked, "*when's the book coming out?*" Well, surprise! Here it is! (LOL)

I'm an incurable romantic. I was born that way, so, it has always been completely natural for me to write love poetics. Over the years, other poets have dared and challenged me to "step outside the box," and do something different, almost as if it is wrong or unjust of me to categorize myself as a love poet. From time to time I'd humor them; but like waves rushing back to the shore, I always returned to what felt right, pure, like home, and that's love.

soul wide shut is a reflection of the relationships that have touched and affected my world. It is a poetic culmination of lessons learned, an extremely personal way of sharing my experiences with love and heartache.

Putting this book together was beneficial in helping me to deal with an emotional time in my life. These poems made me remember that love is everything, and without it we are nothing. They made me remember to keep the faith and not give up on relationships. They helped to re-affirm that although I'm a little bruised, I'm definitely not broken and my heart is still open to love.

When you've finished reading, I hope you'll have some feedback because I'd love to hear from you! You can visit the blog at **soulwideshut.blogspot.com** or send an email to **soul_wide_shut@mchsi.com.** I promise to respond to each comment or inquiry as soon as I possibly can.

Thank you again! Enjoy the read and the ride!

Layne

At the touch of love everyone becomes a poet.
~Plato

soul wide shut

whole soul fully exposed
yet concurrently
[enclosed]

i mean, in its entirety
wide open/wide shut
akin to a sponge
illicitly absorbing the
very essence of you,
leaving no clues that
i am encountering
this vibe for you...

conceptualizing a touch
so intense it brands,
so extreme glass would be
transposed to its
original form of sand,
and begin
slipping thru fingertips
similar to my soul
wide open/wide shut

openly, yet covertly
dipping/flowing
and mating with yours,
while constantly trivializing
our kinnection
in order to make
the obvious
appear invisible.

love-short #1: intrigued

i'm thinking of you tonight
and in all actuality i have
no right to permit my
psyche to contInUoUSly
conjure romantic similes
concerning you+me equaling one

i have no business feeling
something that could
intrinsically mean:
"you are moving me."
i have no business experiencing
anything that could
ultimately lead
to me declaring:
"i can't breathe without you."

and i shouldn't be imagining
how it would be to
completely have you
just for myself...

after all,
i don't even know your name.

dreamcatcher

i felt you today
feeling me/feeling you,
i then wondered if you knew
how my mind
loves to contemplate
the very idea of you, and
what it would be like to
have you lying close to me,
sweetly whispering
all of the sensual things
you'll freely do
if i promise to come for you

my mind loves you,
even as it drifts, continuously
on the iridescent wings of
indiscriminate musings;
do you mind if i fantasize
about the first time we
kissed in the future?

i want you to
gently bite my bottom lip,
before giving me
the perfect kiss, and
permit me to taste
the smile on the tip
of your tongue
as it enters my mouth

my mind loves your invasion,
and all the ways you
systematically shut down

my weakened defenses,
making it nearly impossible
for me to keep even my
daydreams dry...
especially when i imagine
what it must feel like
having you all over
and in(side) me, deliberately
etching your essence
indelibly into my skin

and since my dreams are
simply ethereal wishes
waiting impatiently to be
realized and brought to fruition;
if you are only a hallucination,
or a beautiful figment of my
overactive imagination,
let me just say,
(with absolutely no filters in place)
"i can not wait to meet you."

interlude (the conception)

i don't know him
from the stranger at the
stoplight next to me...
i only have a voice
a vibe, and
virtual smiles to archive,
no face or happy hugs
his love is like
a memory yet to be a birthed,
a song still waiting to be sung

i do not know him, yet
the fact that he
arouses my interest is no secret
(at least not to us), and

i wonder if he understands
he could become a habit that
i'm certain i'll never
be able to break, because
with each poetic breath i take,
i ache for the event
that will allow me the opportunity
to experience his unique brand
of beautiful, once again

i yearn for the chance
to partake of his
intoxicating intellect and strength,
in hopes that both will be
lastingly etched
on my mental palette;

not fleetingly like
lovemaking's afterglow, but
permanent like indigo on skin

i'm dying softly
in anticipation of the occasion
to feel his vibe
co-exist with mine
for an overextended
period of time, and
i'm slowly discovering
the exciting possibilities found
in allowing the mere
thought of someone new
to cause my heart to smile,
and once again have me
thinking in poetics...

so, although he is unexpected,
he is definitely welcome to enter.

i didn't want to call

up at 1am and i am attempting
(ineffectively)
to deny the fact that i am
dying to reach out and
allow his vibe to
fiber-optically entwine and
coalesce with mine
on some divine,
"i'm-diggin'-you-like-this"
type shit...

you see, it's been a long time
since i've pined for the
conversational intimacy
of another or allowed myself
to meditate on what it would
feel like to lie in bed all night,
laughing and whispering about
any/every and no/thing at all,

so, i didn't want to call him.

i knew hearing his voice would
more than likely conjure imagery
of future wet dreams, or
at least facilitate gentle musings
involving much too familiar things
that could range anywhere from
backrubs by candlelight to
make-up kisses after silly fights,

i knew he would probably express
some sweet sentiment that
would effortlessly orchestrate
the fluttering of butterfly wings
in the pit of my stomach, and
in an instant my 5 senses would
multiply 200 thousand times over,
providing 1 million reasons why
i could blissfully listen to him speak
'til the sunlight begins to peak
thru my windowpane,

so, taking into consideration
all of these things,
i didn't want to call him; but
in the end i'm glad i did.

the conversation kiss

he conversation kissed me
for an entire evening,

from my head to my feet
his words wrapped around me,
euphorically, bringing to mind
the passion that permeates
the perfect french kiss...

his sweet-talk caressed
every inch of me thoroughly, and
i selfishly hung on to each
noun/adjective/verb that
dripped from his beautiful lips
and slipped into the deepest depths
of my most erotic musing;
making me yearn to achieve
pure physical intimacy...

but instead,
he conversation kissed me.

his dialogue penetrated, deeply
i was suspended in time,
i could almost feel his mouth
on mine when he articulated
things like:
"i wouldn't want to be
anywhere else tonight."
and he whispered things like:
"i'm certain i've been waiting
for you all of my life."

so, i just closed my eyes,
tilted my head to the side, and
flowed on his vernacular vibe
to mind-blown and back, and

even now when i hear this
brotha speak...
(he doesn't even have to be talking to me)
my heart still misses a beat,
remembering
the first time we kissed.

untitled

have you ever spoken to someone for the
very first time, and all you wanted to
tell them is how much you've missed them?

you get me that way.

you are completely filling my senses, and
we've never even touched,

you are infinitely overwhelming me with
every thing that is brilliant,
all things that are beautiful,
that perfect thing called you...

you make me question my creation, wondering
did i even exist before you came along?

you are increasingly becoming all that i need
or ever dreamed i wanted to know,

you are moving me in ways that surpass the physical:
it's intense,
it's emotional,
it's mental, magnificent...

you are completely filling my senses, and
i've missed you.

the ?uestions (say yes)

if i release my thoughts to you,
will you let them play?

let's say... that i... softly...
set them adrift on the wings
of the many mental vibrations
that permeate from
my souls concentration, and
they without vacillation
gravitated directly to you...
would you willingly
allow them uninterrupted access
into the deepest recess
of your enigmatic essence?

if i were to sweetly unleash
multiple mindgasms
using the passionate energy
created in my
always-prolific dreams
starring you and me...
would they be freely permitted
to traverse thru the universe,
find their way to your
hearts front door, and
boldly implore that you
love me like i love you?

i want you to need me, profoundly
like i need you.

an even swap is never a swindle,
or so it would seem, therefore
it's only fair that we should
arrange for the exchange of
some sort of emotional currency,
with an unconditional
no-love-back guarantee...
after all, i plan on being
wrapped up inside your soul
for countless eternities, so

if i release my thoughts to you,
(and you only)
will you let them play...

please?

guesswork (the royal blak re-mix)

i don't know why i am
continuously set adrift with
each and every sonic snap my
heart rim-shots when it skips
its rhythm in his presence,

i don't know why, but i
sometimes wonder if he
is mythological, then when
he part my lips with tongue kisses
it becomes apparent that he is
equivalent to my happiness,

i don't know why i prefer to
inscribe him into my soul with
metaphysical metaphors euphoric, or
why when i look into his eyes
i lose my breath, i am left
speechless and my totally blown mind
desperately races to find
where he could have possibly
hidden my heart,

i don't know why when he
says my name it's like
i'm hearing music
for the very first time, and
i wish i'd been blessed with
musical genius, so i could
effortlessly orchestrate
a concerto in the key of him,

i don't know why he is
mastering me, and
it doesn't really matter...
all i know is he breathes
within my inhales and exhales
ever-present effervescence,

his essence is love personified,
it touched me somewhere,
i don't know when, but it did,
i felt it, and
i don't know why...

enchanted (by you)

maybe i should set my emotions free
on the wings of a gentle summer breeze,
releasing them discreetly to the universe
while praying nobody sees
they originated with me,

'cause...

i don't want to bore you with my
asinine introspective comments,
nor do i wish to bother you with
senseless mental gibberish, since
rambling would only serve to
draw attention to what is currently
my best kept secret,

and that is...

every time i witness your beautiful
brand of intelligence, whenever
i make contact with your ubiquitous
spiritual energy, it is absolutely captivating,
that's when it becomes crystal clear to me
i am being completely enchanted,

and it's purely a personal predicament,
so, i don't want to bore you with it...

not when my primary objective is to
prevent myself from telling you
(over and over and over again)

there's something about you that
seamlessly elicits everlasting
smiles in me,

there's something about your
unadulterated adorability that
instantly gets to me, and
in spite of everything
i am being completely enchanted,

effortlessly...

more and more.

under arrest (an addiction peace)

it's as if he spoke directly to my soul
and told it to:
"freeze! hold it right there!
get your hands in the air, and
assume the position of lost in love,"

because he's got me feeling like
i'm under emotional arrest...
and altho' i know this divulgence
can and probably will be
held against me,
i have to admit, truthfully, i have
become his acquiescent captive

he strip-searched me passionately
and confiscated my heart,
leaving me willing to be incarcerated
romantically, for the cause (of love),
without pause, longing to be locked up,
and i'm going down (eagerly),
with no desire for an early release

i don't even want to be considered
for parole, 'cause truth be told...
the members of the board couldn't
possibly understand, just how
good it is being loved by this man, and
for the life of me i couldn't pretend
to even be slightly reformed,

i've been imprisoned by his essence
far too long,

(and i like it here)

so, i'll just stay and bravely face my
twenty-to-life, realizing...
i do have the right to remain silent,
wholeheartedly under his
affectionate arrest, especially since
i've already confessed to
premeditatedly loving him to death.

fulfilled (a tanka for him)

he says he's lonely
but i want to fill his void
and overwhelm him
softly, with the love of me
until he wants nothing more

poetic confession

i tend to think the elusive
is obtainable
whenever we speak...
your words are always
tinged with laughter,
they linger on my mental,
caress my chi, and
cause my heart to smile

did you know my entire world
is brightened considerably
when you allow me to
be/come a muse for you?

you tend to dispel my disbeliefs
while touching me
in places i thought before
were out of reach, and
i am completely smitten with
your cleverness and wit

we tend to lose track of time
standing still,
absorbing
every verb and tense,
easily making
meaningful sentences out of
the sweetest nonsense

this tendency we have
of touching/holding anything,
reaching toward something,

hoping for everything,
all the while wondering
what if...

makes me question how much
longer i can hide behind the guise
of aloofness and disinterest, or
pretend to speculate on the elusive
before i take a chance, and
tell you

...i am falling.

gentle persuasion

if he were an
opulent ocean
lying calmly
before me,
i would instantaneously
dive into him
heart first,
eyes open wide,
forgoing the need
to hold my breath,
forgetting to remember
to brace myself,
i would unhurriedly
submerge into his
deepest depths
in an honest attempt
to inundate my self
and drench my spirit
in all of his
vast magnificence,
i'd then air dry
so that i
could fully experience
his sweet essence
sensuously soaking
into every pore
of my skin,
caressing the very core
of my existence,
making me want to
get wet again.

acquiescence (senryu)

it blows my mind, but
i can no longer deny:
i'm in love with you.

you got me

this morning i saw a resplendent
orange moon, and
my mental instantaneously caressed
amorous thoughts of you...

and i was driving silently,
all the while wondering if
you know i flow freely, creaming
at your ability to infiltrate me
souldeep then send me
reeling/feeling/wanting
nothing but you...

i mean, this experience is
so intense that i don't know if
i'm going or coming,
coming or going to cum
at the thought of your tongue
leaving lingering love licks on
every unadorned inch of
my exposed 6-ft countenance
and get this:
you haven't even touched me yet
(at least not in the physical sense)

and still—
i am feeling you like this.

beautiful black man...
my sun/my muse,
your moon is so into you, and
i like it here...

so, do you mind if i stay
in this place, gently inhabiting
your up close and personal space,
while forever marveling at the way
your heartbeat keeps perfect
pitter-pat pace with mine?
and the entire time
i'm left open w i d e,
no longer able to hide this
never-ending desire to fuck you...

actually, i'm willing to let you
blow on my coffee,
lie in my coveted bed
beside me/inside me,
arriving with me continuously,

i want to tell you secret things
and saturate your god-like mentality
in my southern sensuality...
you can even have the extra key
that unlocks every thing dear to me,
'cause i am loving you like that,

admittedly, you... got... me.

don't let go (love)

from the first moment
your ever-present essence
began haunting my every
waking dream it seems
you have been my focus:
the constant center
of my hearts attention,
the foundation that
fortifies my fulfillment,
the axis on which my
world wondrously rests, and
my love will never do
without you, so...

when butterflies and emptiness
infuse my soul
on those singular
sunday mornings spent
sipping coffee
without you, and
when i feel cold on those
solitary autumn evenings
spent sleepless with
Miles and no you,
i realize loneliness has
literally become the
unfortunate prerequisite
to my impending
contentment, so...

my primary point-of-view
consistently stays on
anticipating you, and

the day when we'll be
in the same place,
at the same time...

but, 'til that moment arrives:
i need your energy surrounding me,
i need you as close as
the sound of your voice
seemingly allows you to be,
more than flowers, cards
or trivial material things...
i need you always,
in all ways, remembering
our emergent feelings
are everything, so please,
don't let go of this love.

you: the poem

you got me saturated in
the sounds of Coltrane
and falling rain, licking
flavored coffee off lips that
desperately wish
for the taste of you,

you got me set adrift on
melancholy bliss, wondering
why i'm suddenly so amiss,
here in this place where i've
managed to exist, content
for months on end,

then again that was before
you came right on time, and
why every word in this poem
is gonna be about you.

my world was not ready for you...
i apologize that i'm having to
tidy up my space while you
reside in it, but see, i had no clue
you were coming,

(a call, an email or a text message
would have been divine)

now, i'm steadily coming to grips
with having absolutely no grasp
on my emotions or my predicament.

so, what do i say to you when
i'm digging you to such an
intense extent, i've become
reacquainted with
the age-old approach of
waiting by the phone?

i didn't know love would manifest
inside of me through your
simple and intimate linguist
tongue tricks, and
i had no idea my heart
would become dependent on
the mere acknowledgement
of your perfect existence,

so, every word, every line,
every phrase in this poem
is gonna be about you, and
how you've managed to
inspire me effortlessly, and
without an ounce of difficulty
left the part of you
that breathes in me.

between us

you are my constant:
like the threehundredsixty
ceaselessly existing
invariable degrees
of a perpetual
platinum circle...
no ending/no beginning
incessantly unremitting
flawlessly continuous

you are the one thing
in my crazy world
that remains the same
forever unchanged, and
we love in depths that are
deeper than oceans, and
as limitless as the
heavens are high

a day without you
would be to me like
a day without
sunshine or butterflies, and
although it's true
i could exist without you
in my life, honestly,
i hope i never have to

jokes and shameless
flirtation aside,
from the moment our
vibes initially entwined

you have been my constant
time after time after time,
consistently...

(hey you)

have i told you recently
just how precious you are to me?

no complaints: for the extraordinary muse

he's got that extra-special everything
that keeps me extra-intrigued, and
i won't lie/i could lie in
his presence and get extra-high
by absorbing his
extra-spectacular essence,
on any given day/any given night,

he makes me write extra-sweet
love shit in an effort to convey
the way he moves me, extra-easily
to the pulsating beat
of his extra-unique rhythm,

he's got those extra-exclusive gifts
that give my heart and soul an
extra-ultimate lift, then steals my
breath from me, in a way that's
extra-astounding, and

i won't lie/i could lie in
his extra-gentle embrace, and
allow him to extra-carefully erase
every single trace of craziness
i had to face before he made
his extra-impressive entrance,

i guess what i'm trying to say is:
he's got an extra-incredible way
of making everything around me
appear to be extra-lovely, and
i can't lie/i could lie extra-content
by his side for
extra-infinite lifetimes,
that's how extra-ordinary
he is
to me...

lovejonesin' (there's definitely a reason why)

you be that
cherryblueblackstrawberry
aphrodisiac that effortlessly
brings my soul alive, and
resuscitates my hearts desire
to write you love poems,
sing you love songs,
or just to be loved by you, and
if i had my way, i would
make your bornday a
national holiday, 'cause
i just want to celebrate
the moment
you took your first breath,
made your first sound,
or first made someone happy

(and just like me, your folks had
to be overjoyed at your arrival)

brotha, you be that
sweet cream in my coffee
or at least the concoction that
makes me cream sweetly, and
it seems i never knew love
until you came along...
now i'm absolutely turned out,
completely strung out,
or entirely spaced out

(you make the call)

just the other day...
you touched me,
you kissed me,
or maybe you just breathed
but you sent me, floating
past cloud 9, and
hanging from 9 was an
OUT OF BUSINESS sign
that said lovers should contact you
to learn how to get lifted

(you be bad like that)

so, keeping in mind that this
ain't no line,
no players diatribe,
or no game cleverly designed
to gas you up,
(no matter how it might sound)
i just want you to be
my three-sixty-five valentine,
my for all time,
or my 'til the end of time, cause i'm
entirely convinced when i say this:
"love doesn't exist without you."

heaven (i love your peace)

observing you at perfect peace,
as you speak/write/think/sleep;
when you snuggle up to me
as you dream, or awaken me
slow and sweet with
strategically placed butterfly kisses
on the back of my neck,

the way you hold me tight
during late night thunderstorms, or
caress the worry lines
from my forehead
'til my self-imposed
"i-need-to-be-superwoman" mentality
is gone,

long easy sundays spent
laughing about our differences, yet
finding consolation in the fact
we have all the important
matters in common, then there's

sharing french vanilla coffee
while raindrops fall softly,
scented candles flickering
as we hold hands and
say grace in two-part harmony,
or make love and arrive
(at the same time)
on the other side of divine,

amalgamating your vibe with mine
while bringing my
conscious soul alive,
politicking passionately about
how we'll successfully
raise our seed, and
still manage to leave
precious poetic legacies
as priceless gifts to the masses,

romantic meditations and
aspirations of grandeur
notwithstanding,
you are simply my truth...
and being given the chance
to go through life with you
is heaven to me.

synonyms of diggin' him (the conscious version)

sixhundredseventy days down
and counting, still
i'm diggin' you like—

an old soul record that stays
in maximum rotation on
every radio station
across the nation, making
everyone who hears it
reminisce and say shit like:
"ooooo, that's my song!"
as they wave their hands, and
hum along to timeless lyrics
that make them secretly wish
they could write love poems

the passionate confessions
you whispered during intense
politicking sessions no longer
leave me questioning whether
your actions could possibly be as
spectacular as your words—
i am a devout believer, and
you are my new religion...
ever since you began
gently laying hands, and
continuously baptizing me
in your unique brand of
revolutionary-blunted
black-on-black love, undiluted

now, i got you...
all up in my peace, and
i'm still diggin' you—

reaching even higher, emotionally
as you incessantly
french kiss me, deep
with the essence of always
on the tip if your tongue, intentionally
leaving the sweetest trace
of exclusivity on my mouth...
so that when i lick my lips,
nearly two years later, all i taste
is forever laced with you

waiting in vain

it's been 2 days 22 hours
8 minutes and 7 seconds since
i was last afforded the opportunity
to be near you, and
this is not, at all, what i've grown
accustomed to, so
my heart is telling my head
it's actually been an eternity

you see

i am missing you…
in every shade of blue imaginable
and i keep checking the calendar
to be sure it hasn't been
2 years 22 months
8 weeks and 7 days since
i was thrown into this emotional maze
that's got me in a daze, because
i can't feel my way thru the haze
that's keeping you from me

you seem to think, i'm being
"sweet and understanding", and
really, i have no alternative, since
i can't leave; it's too late for that…
besides, who else is going to
have your back while you work thru
this shit you're dealing with?

you see

i don't want to add to your stress;
but (and there's always a "but")
i need to hear from you...
maybe then i can make my heart
understand the rules of engagement
as they relate to waiting in the wings
while wondering, without worrying,
if you need me like i need you, or

maybe i'm simply waiting in vain?

musing by moonlight

i am blue in green this evening,
repetitiously summoning
mind-blowing metaphors, and
souldeep similes of things
concerning us 2 arriving at 1, and
my nights without your
countenance upon my back
make my sleepy retreats heavy
with burdensome loneliness,

can you tell that i'm really missing you?
(*i'm really missing you.*)

you have become my
constant muse-of-choice, and
my over-flowing stream of thought
seems to be inundating the
pristine white pages of my
confidential poetry with
brown/deep/you feelings, and
these faceless nights without
your smile to give them
identity and meaning, silently
haunt me

i am blue in green, swaying
with the gently breeze, viewing
the moon thru the trees, with
Miles in my ears and you
at the center of my soul, effortlessly
taking control of my heart, which

by the way, i should say, has decided
to beat only for the love of you, and
there ain't a damn thing i can do

other than tell you
i'm really missing you...
(*i'm really missing you.*)

come home soon.

unspoken allusion: come see about me

he tells me constantly that his
love for me runs exceedingly deep,
he says my essence has
managed to creep into every
aperture of his being and that
i have captured him completely

now, don't get me wrong…
i think all of that is amazing and sweet,
but in this instant, i can barely breathe.
i mean, at night i can't sleep,
during the day, it's hard to concentrate,
and all the times in-between
i simply feel empty,
so, right now i need him
to come and see about me

the urgency of this situation
is like a national emergency, in my mind,
and i'm searching to find a way to convey
to him that i will not be "alright," until i
have him in my sight and can feel
the warmth from his body
wrapping around mine in that way
that whispers:
"you're loved/you're home."

i will not be "just fine," until i
can look into his dark soulful eyes
and actually feel as if time has
decided to stand still, in order to

allow him the opportunity to
infiltrate and heal my aching spirit

it's like, he's the source of the flame
that ignites everything especially
spectacular within me... you know...
all those little things that others
don't always "get" or find significant, and
i want him to come see about me

i'm not overly concerned with
how he gets here...
(just as long as he gets here)
i don't give a damn about
doing my hair, or
what i'm going to wear, 'cause
all the superficial shit will
cease to exist, from the moment
he walks thru the door, stretches
his arms wide/takes me inside,
places my head upon his chest, and
in the soothing voice of love says:
*"i felt you needed me, so
i came to see about you."*

as they lay

fingertips touching fingertips
his lips exploring her softer lips
as they lay
hips dipping into fuller hips, and

he didn't even try to
slip inside;
extremely satisfied to lie
between brown thighs
and tangibly memorize
the sublime sensations
associated with
being cradled so close to
heavens entrance

hands gently caressing faces
her legs encircling his waist
as they lay
moans colliding with sighs, and

she didn't even want to
close her eyes;
so completely mesmerized
by the quixotic fire
that glowed from the windows
of his beautiful soul
seductively whispering
the age-old anecdote of desires
waiting to be realized, and

time tip-toed by
as they lay

entwined in
reciprocal propinquity,

he tongue-kissing her collarbone
as breaths coalesce passionately,
she lightly-licking his earlobe
as love words are spoken softly,

just before they
drift off to sleep,
both of them
clothed completely.

succulent

each and every time i see his face
i mindlessly concentrate on his
perfectly shaped/erotically made
much too luscious not to lick
totally flawless/beautiful lips, and

i am losing control of the ability
to think coherently
on anything other than
how i am desperately seeking
the opportunity to give in
and live in his kiss

staring at his lips has me
anxiously yearning for their taste,
lustfully counting the innumerable ways
they'll cause my heart to race when
they begin to lovingly trace
my body and face
leaving remarkable impressions
of him on me

in my wettest dreams, i outline
his lips with my fingertip, then
boldly replace it with my tongue,
and he uses his eyes to mentally
transcribe thoughts of wickedly kissing
the essence of my femininity
with long/slow/deep familiarity,
until those beautiful lips are
glossed and stained with my
unrestrained fluidity

"but these words are just vibrations of
air until they are attached to reality"

so in actuality, i won't be content
until i can tangibly commit the
taste/touch/feel of those lips
to memory, in hopes of creating
everlasting reminiscences of
kissing/kisses/being kissed in
places i once considered off limits
and highly restricted, then

every part of me will forever be
passion-marked with:
RESERVED FOR HIS BEAUTIFUL LIPS ONLY.

erotically thinking

it gets hard sometimes...
(no pun intended)
thinking about being in love
without considering
how pleasurable it would be
having you on/in me, with
me flowing beneath you,
with us two moving in perfect sync
to a groove as intrinsic
and uninhibited as an
afrikan tribal dance

(and in my musings we
do get "natural" like that)

you be mischievously
tugging on nappy hair,
deliberately ripping pretty underwear,
audaciously bending me(over)
to your will,
shamelessly kissing and licking
on everything...
leaving no doubt in my mind
about just how low you're
willing to go to please me, and
it's at this time that i
feel inclined to let you know:
(in-between shallow breaths)
payback, is indeed, a bitch
and i got next...

i be possessively
cradling you between brown thighs,
repeatedly calling on The Most High,
defiantly trying not to cry(out)
since big girls DO NOT do that shit!
besides, i can't have you
erroneously assuming
i want you to stop...
at least not until
we both get enough
or get lifted
or get tired and fall asleep
or until i wake from ruminating
to make this poem a reality

(whichever comes first)

closer

exalting in the fortuity
to experience you
uninterrupted,
lying unadorned in your
on-time embrace,
thigh to thigh
breasts pressed to chest
skin touching skin
increasingly/rhythmically
breathing you in,
my mental finding it
difficult to comprehend
where i end and you begin,
hearts beat in sync
souls become twins
vibes interweave
oneness achieved,
so close are we
in proximity and still
i yearn to be closer.

he made tiny circles

he made tiny circles with his tongue
around my outer ear, whispering
soft and clear, exactly what he would
do to me, if i promised i'd try to lie
relatively motionless and allow him the
chance to worship me, freely

he made tiny circles with his tongue
down the sensitive left side of my neck,
across my collarbone and my chest,
til' those sweet circles brought his mouth
into direct contact with nipple, right

and i wanted to scream that he was
so damn wrong for making me
moan his name and forcing me
to commit total blasphemy when
i repeatedly called him *"my god!"*

those tiny circles slowly traveled
down my side, skipping my hip
since it was being lovingly gripped
by his warm brown hand...

wait a minute. let me start again.

those tiny wet circles traversed down
my side, meticulously finding their way
to smooth brown thighs that
(on their own accord) parted W I D E
in an attempt to unconsciously direct

the exact destination of this
circuitous attack, then with

intentions met, their target found,
the tiny circles roamed
'round and 'round and 'round, slowly
circumnavigating the slick/hot/wet center
of my queenly existence;
from a distance i heard a scream, and
surprisingly realized it was me
seamlessly be/coming undone...

then the pressure of the tiny circles
increased/decreased/disappeared
(in conjunction with big licks)
and i lay there, eyes closed tightly,
spinning off my damn axis,
(panting)
spiraling off my damn axis,
(relaxing)
until permission to return to earth
was finally granted.

satiated

drained
replete
spent
i thought i felt the earth tilt
throughout the amalgamating,

exhales
drenched
aquatic in our movements
love refrains muttered in sensual utterances
in-between tongue dances and melanin tangos

powerful
deep
spine-tingling
i took your fingers into my mouth, then
used them to write your name on my skin,
along with the whispered chant:
i was made for you.
we were made for this.

quiet
dark
unadorned
you are the outline of my satisfied body
you are the outline of my satisfied body

(kiss)
light conversation
(kiss)

staring into eyes
(kiss)
limbs entwined
(kiss)

spooned from behind
finally
asleep.

loveshort #2: naïve

i am remembering—
fingertips gently pressed
against a mouth
sweetly swollen
from passionate kisses
sinfully stolen
in covetous moments
spent with
a king who wasn't mine
a king whose soul was
ceremonially entwined and
promised to a wife
but i, being both
foolish and blind
thought that i
could have him
for myself, so
i ignored all the signs
naïvely closed my eyes
and refused to
make my captive heart
realize that
i was definitely
loving
on borrowed time.

truth is (a working title)

it is easy to love the laughter,
too effortless to love the laughter:
i love you even when it's gone

during world-class shouting matches
filled with foul-mouthed fluencies
that tear thru the air, reverberating
off our sanctuary walls like
heartbreakingly argumentative,
emotion-filled bullets
(wounding the spirit when they penetrate
precisely at the intended point of entry)

or when the silence in the room is
so mean, loud and thick that it
clings to our clothes like
wisps of copious smoke from
egyptian musk incense, or
lingers on brown skin like
the subtle afterthought of an
extremely expensive fragrance
(in other words it tends to hover
for hours and hours on end)

but then again...

it is easy to love the calm,
too uncomplicated to love the calm:
i love you even when it's gone

maybe that's because it's an
undisputed fact, the painful lack

of tranquility won't subsist for long,
it simply never does, and
maybe that's because we don't deny
both you and i are fallible, imperfect
ugly and ill-tempered, at times, yet
we are all ways each other's one

it is easy to love the sun,
much too easy to love the sun:
i love you even when it's gone

when blue/black storm clouds
shroud our peaceful co-existence
bringing rain that hangs around, for days
and our happily-ever-after notions
are tested, assessed
and then
tested once more,
the unpretentious truth is:
i still adore you...

and i'll never need another.

if

i. prerequisite

if i could wrap the world
in a brilliant silver bow, and
if i knew where to go to
capture sunglow, moonbeams
or any other heavenly thing
your sweet heart desired,
i'd do it without hesitation
(if you wanted me to) and
even if you didn't actually
request it, but somehow i thought
you'd bless the attempt, the
endeavor would gladly become
mine to pursue

ii. qualifications

if heartbeats depended solely
on the deep resonance of
mellifluous male voices,
if souls were meant to be
penetrated deep by the
mere act of sensual hand-to-skin
contact, and
if perfectly placed kisses were
to suddenly become life sustaining
instruments, i'd have no choice,
except to publicly admit:
you are my every thing

iii. stipulations

if only infinite alternatives truly existed,
if this wish-full thinking
that i constantly experience would
cease to persist, and
if i could at long last, have you
all to myself, i'd love to tell you that
my mind never stops imagining the
definitive thought of you and me...

iv. disclaimer

but unfortunately,
there are just too many "ifs"
between us

disappearing acts

this is for the man who
inspired my fire
that once resided
in him

the man

who has become another
poem in my past, and
at the same time
made me realize that
my best poetics
will be written
in future-tense

the man

who made me laugh from
inside jokes,
allowed me to lament
over the pain
of lost family and friends, and
listened to me sleep
on nights when
our kinnection seemed
much too deep
to entertain the
idea of saying anything
remotely resembling
good-bye

the man

beautiful, heart-melting voice
(especially when
speaking my name),
his love changed me,
made me sing love songs
out loud, and
live to embrace the belief
that destiny is indubitably
an authentic entity

the man

who deliberately left
his fingerprints
on my heart, along with
the subtle hint of
happiness experienced
when time was spent
getting to know him, and

i am missing him like we never met.

mood indigo (the blues)

on the canvas of your mind,
imagine you can see
what i'm feeling inside:
intensely powerful sentiments
in every shade of blue from
cobalt to sky
sapphire to cerulean
royal to navy
turquoise to baby
powder to periwinkle
swirling/twirling/blending
with overtones of
black and gray...
culminating and climaxing
to create a
masterpiece of misery
overwhelmed by longing
filled with regret
consumed by fear
wracked with pain, entirely
forcing the acknowledgement
that forgiveness
is not guaranteed.

poetic letter #41 (atonement)

hey you,

okay. so, now you know the whole story, and in all actuality, i thought i'd feel better, freer, lighter, calmer, once i'd finally divulged some of the most intimate details of my life to you. but, i don't.

truth be told, i feel more embarrassed than ever before about having to openly admit, to you of all people, i was involved in that farce of a matrimonial commitment. i feel like crying. i feel like hiding. for the first time, in a long time, i feel like giving up. throwing in the towel. calling it quits, and simply letting go of any asinine ideas i'd covertly conceived concerning, you and me, ever being anything more than perfunctory passers-by, who only superficially touched each others lives.

during the course of our four hour politicking session, the conversation, understandably got a little intense. yet, i wholeheartedly welcomed the chance to attempt to express myself, unfiltered.

you have no idea how it feels to talk to you sometimes. i know what i want to say, but i end up holding it inside, because i know that in the front of your mind, every word that leaves my lips is being received and weighed as disingenuous. but, for a long while during our exchange, it felt like the total opposite. it was kind of like the "good old days", for a moment. but, i knew i couldn't get too relaxed because...

in the words of that Lauren Hill track: "*no matter how i think we grow, you always seem to let me know, it ain't workin'.*" by now, i expect it, yet it still stings. it hurts. it sucks ass... BIG time. and what do i do? i keep right on trying. i give you space, time, respect your wishes to be left alone... for weeks on end, then i do it again. (sigh) hoping that the next time, will be the charmed time, and you'll miraculously decide i really am trust/worthy enough for you to let me come closer. (sigh, again.)

now, i'm an advocate of reciprocation, so it's no fun being the one who's always initiating interaction. but hey, i guess those are the breaks when i'm the only one who seems to care.

so today, i realized, maybe i need to find a damn clue. maybe i need to make peace with the fact i just cannot win with you, and it's time to fuckin' fold 'em, you know?

you seem to think it's the love of a "challenge" that keeps me constantly running into the brick wall of your stubbornness, emotional indifference, and resolve, and that might be 33.3% true. in any event, please believe it's not out of a sense of guilt, for things done in the past, or some kind of misplaced moral commitment.

it's just because no matter what anyone else thinks or says, or even when i kick my own ass for being a masochist and a glutton for punishment, the truth is... i still miss and adore you. and ultimately, it matters **to me**, what **you** think **of me** and that's merely real-talk.

in the spirit of absolute accountability (i know you're big on that), i have no one to blame for my shit, but me. this whole situation is reminiscent of a poem by nikki g. called, "he blew it." and altho' she was speaking on something completely different than the dynamics of "our thing," the title still rings true. i know; i blew it. fucked up. made a mess of something that started out, honestly, devoid of any cruel intent. the sad thing is, i could live and try 36 more years and i'd probably never convince you of that.

you've declared in postscript that **everything**, with me, was always so intricate, "difficult" to be exact. i wish i shared your sentiment; however, i can't, since i didn't see it like that. maybe i'm just romanticizing our shit? still, i know you used the word l-o-v-e, too, and in my mind, what i felt for you was never arduous. as a matter of fact, it saved me. protected my souls sanity. made me believe in the existence of infinite possibilities (again), and for that, alone, i thank you, unconditionally.

so, i guess that's it. please promise me you won't let thoughts of ill-fated kismet (especially for me and things i never confessed), steal your future dreams? i think you deserve to have everything you want...

alwayspeace,

me

sometimes

sometimes i catch myself
trying to comprehend how and when
we got lost in this storm.
i wonder/ponder/question
where the hell we went wrong
amid a long list of future dreams
and forever-after thinking
that eventually flew away like
dead winter leaves,
caught in the vortex
of a vicious spring breeze

and

sometimes my internal dialogue
conjures conclusions that tend to
outweigh the evident; for instance,

when i'm lonely in bed at night
i imagine that you and i will
finally find a way to be
righteous together, then
i realize, i should know better
because the truth of the matter is
i've never been worth the risk,
and you've never truly
needed me
with quite the same urgency
that i have for you

and

sometimes it seems
sweet release is only
a moment away, then
on other days, letting go feels like
it will take infinity to perpetuate

and

i'm not sure why, but
more than likely it's
derivative of the fact that
regardless of the pain
someone caused in the past,
in spite of the heartache
they initiated on your behalf,
sometimes you'll simply love
some people your entire life.

re: affirmation (love's still all right)

last night i lay awake,
heart and soul open wide
with no need for
pretense or pride, and
i cried for everything we
should have been
could have done
would have experienced, as one

i cried for all the love we
should have shared
could have felt
would have made, together
i cried from deep within, and
i don't remember when
sleep at last claimed
my consciousness, but

i do know this, that it's true
what i heard someone say one day,
something like:
"weeping may endure for the night;
but joy comes in the morning time"

because after all the
tears/heartache/frustration, wasted
on someone who obviously
didn't deserve me in the first place
have passed away,
i find myself being thankful
for the journey,

(bruised; but not broken)
i see the promise of
new beginnings/new experiences
and a brand new day, shining
divinely bright...
and in my heart resides hope,
so i know...
love still moves
love still breathes
love's still all right.